FUN FACT FILE:
THE HISTORY OF HOLIDAYS
20 FUN FACTS ABOUT JUNETEENTH
AF594702
BY JILL KEPPELER
Gareth Stevens
PUBLISHING

Please visit our website, www.garethstevens.com. For a free color catalog of all our high-quality books, call toll free 1-800-542-2595 or fax 1-877-542-2596.

Library of Congress Cataloging-in-Publication Data
Names: Keppeler, Jill, author.
Title: 20 fun facts about Juneteenth / Jill Keppeler. Other titles: Twenty fun facts about Juneteenth
Description: New York : Gareth Stevens Publishing, [2025] |
Series: Fun fact file : the history of holidays | Includes bibliographical references and index.
Identifiers: LCCN 2024001383 (print) | LCCN 2024001384 (ebook) | ISBN 9781482466225 (library binding) | ISBN 9781482466218 (paperback) | ISBN 9781482466232 (ebook)
Subjects: LCSH: Juneteenth–Juvenile literature. | African Americans–Texas–History–Juvenile literature. | Enslaved persons–Emancipation–United States–Juvenile literature. | African Americans–Anniversaries, etc.–Juvenile literature.
Classification: LCC E185.93.T4 K47 2025 (print) | LCC E185.93.T4 (ebook) | DDC 394.263–dc23/eng/20240214
LC record available at https://lccn.loc.gov/2024001383
LC ebook record available at https://lccn.loc.gov/2024001384

First Edition

Published in 2025 by
Gareth Stevens Publishing
2544 Clinton St
Buffalo, NY 14224

Editor: Therese Shea

Photo credits: Cover, pp. 1 (main), 29 Svet foto/Shutterstock.com; file folder used throughout David Smart/Shutterstock.com; binder clip used throughout luckyraccoon/Shutterstock.com; wood grain background used throughout ARENA Creative/Shutterstock.com; pp. 5, 22 Tippman98x/Shutterstock.com; p. 6 Everett Collection/Shutterstock.com; p. 7 Invision Frame/Shutterstock.com; pp. 8, 11 courtesy of the Library of Congress; p. 9 Emancipation Day Celebration band, June 19, 1900 (cropped).png/Wikimedia Commons; p. 10 General Order 3/National Archives Catalog; p. 12 AmCyc Houston - market and opera house.jpg/Wikimedia Commons; p. 13 travelview/Shutterstock.com; p. 14 Esc Leo/Shutterstock.com; p. 15 EWY Media/Shutterstock.com; p. 16 FourthWardshotgunshacks.jpg/ Wikimedia Commons; p. 17 Emancipation Day celebration - 1900-06-19.jpg/Wikimedia Commons; p. 18 Prostock-studio/ Shutterstock.com; p. 19 Juneteenth Celebration at Emancipation Park, 1880.png/Wikimedia Commons; p. 20 Linda Hughes Photography/Shutterstock.com; p. 21 Guajillo studio/Shutterstock.com; p. 21 (inset) Eduardo Lopez/Shutterstock.com; p. 23 Maglara/ Shutterstock.com; p. 24 Al Edwards Statue.jpg/Wikimedia Commons; pp. 25, 27 The White House/flickr; p. 26 mark reinstein/ Shutterstock.com.

Printed in the United States of America

CPSIA compliance information: Batch #CS25GS: For further information contact Gareth Stevens, New York, New York at 1-800-542-2595.

CONTENTS

Words in the glossary appear in **bold** type the first time they are used in the text.

A CELEBRATION OF FREEDOM

Juneteenth is a time to gather with family and friends, to dance and sing, and to honor African American **culture**. It's also a time to remember the end of slavery in the United States.

Some holidays have roots going back hundreds of years. Juneteenth is newer. It became a federal, or national, holiday in 2021. It all started in 1865, shortly after the end of the American Civil War. This was the war between the United States and the Southern states that separated from the country, which called themselves the Confederacy.

People may mark Juneteenth with music, dancing, faith services, speeches, parades, and family parties. It's a fun **celebration**, but there are serious events to remember.

THE ROOTS OF THE HOLIDAY

FUN FACT: 1

THE EMANCIPATION PROCLAMATION WAS JUST THE BEGINNING OF THE END OF U.S. SLAVERY.

The end of slavery began with an official statement, or proclamation, by President Abraham Lincoln. It said all enslaved people in areas fighting against the United States would be freed, or emancipated, on January 1, 1863.

This painting shows the reading of the Emancipation Proclamation to Lincoln's advisers.

FUN FACT: 2

IN AUGUST 1863, LINCOLN SAID THE EMANCIPATION PROCLAMATION WAS THE "HEAVIEST BLOW YET" TO THE CONFEDERACY.

The war had been about keeping the United States together. After the proclamation, it became a war about ending slavery. The Emancipation Proclamation also announced Black men could join the U.S. military.

This image shows Black Americans on December 31, 1862, waiting for midnight when the Emancipation Proclamation took effect. Some people today still attend watch night services marking "Freedom's Eve" on New Year's Eve.

FUN FACT: 3

THERE WAS NO SINGLE DAY THAT ALL STATES STOPPED PRACTICING SLAVERY, BUT CELEBRATIONS POPPED UP AS THE NEWS SPREAD.

News of the Emancipation Proclamation spread slowly. U.S. soldiers told people about it as they gained territory. Not everyone heard. Some kept it from the people they enslaved.

TIMELINE OF THE FIRST JUNETEENTH

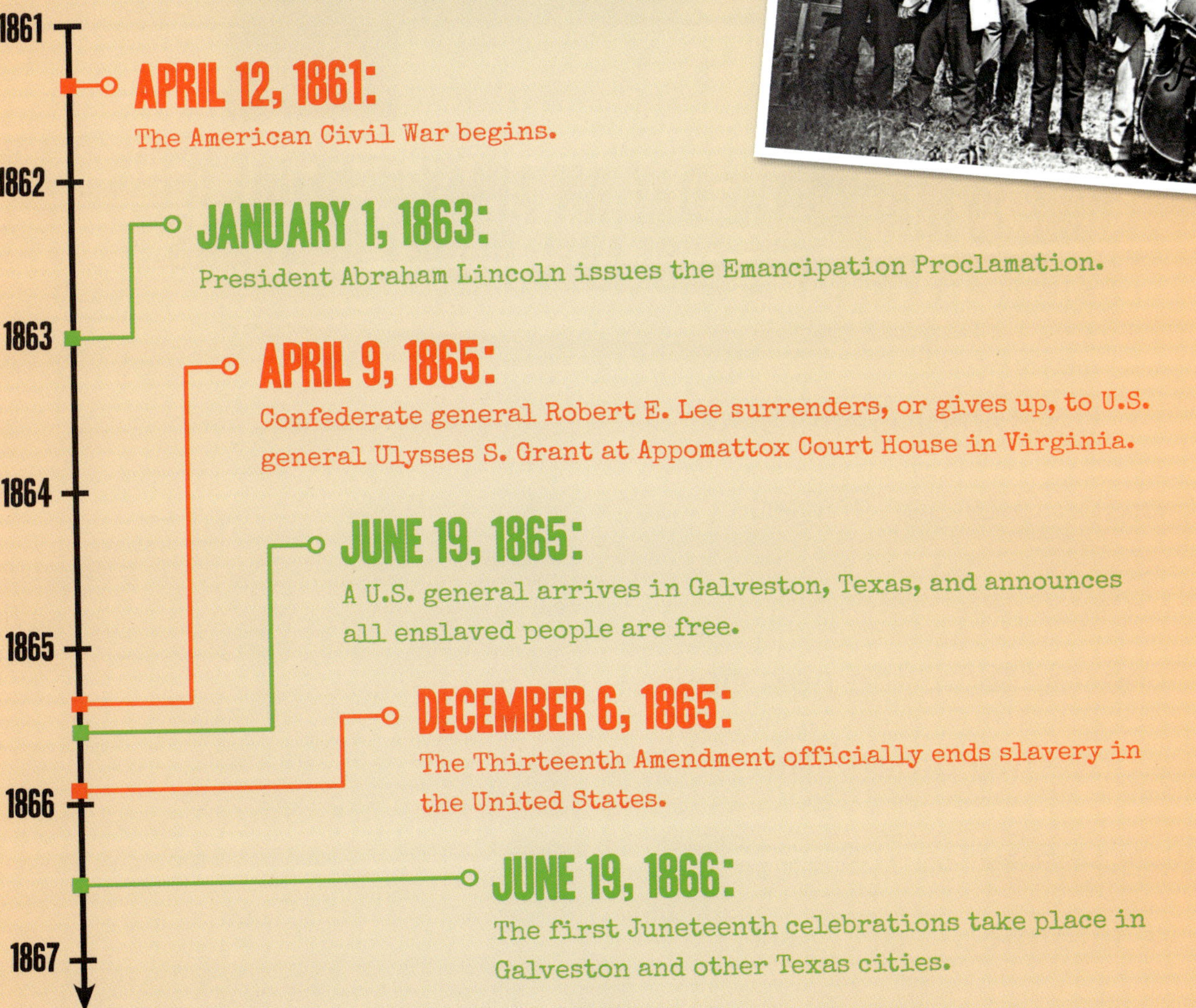

APRIL 12, 1861:
The American Civil War begins.

JANUARY 1, 1863:
President Abraham Lincoln issues the Emancipation Proclamation.

APRIL 9, 1865:
Confederate general Robert E. Lee surrenders, or gives up, to U.S. general Ulysses S. Grant at Appomattox Court House in Virginia.

JUNE 19, 1865:
A U.S. general arrives in Galveston, Texas, and announces all enslaved people are free.

DECEMBER 6, 1865:
The Thirteenth Amendment officially ends slavery in the United States.

JUNE 19, 1866:
The first Juneteenth celebrations take place in Galveston and other Texas cities.

IT STARTED IN TEXAS

FUN FACT: 4

JUNE 19 MARKS THE DAY AN ARMY GENERAL ISSUED AN ORDER TO FREE THE ENSLAVED PEOPLE OF TEXAS.

U.S. Major General Gordon Granger arrived in Galveston, Texas, on June 18, 1865. The next day, he gave five orders. The third one said, "The people are **informed** that . . . all slaves are free."

General Order No. 3 was printed in the Galveston newspaper and read out loud in many places.

About 179,000 Black men served in the U.S. Army by the end of the Civil War.

FUN FACT: 5

GRANGER LIKELY WASN'T THE FIRST TO ANNOUNCE THE NEWS OF FREEDOM, THOUGH.

A week before Granger and his soldiers arrived, a Union force of Black soldiers had captured Galveston. They chased the Confederate forces into Mexico. Thousands of enslaved people escaped.

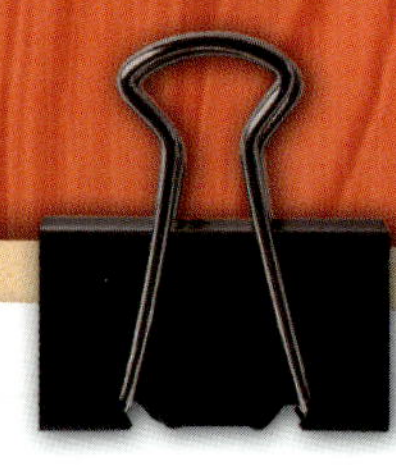

FUN FACT: 6

TEXAS IS A HUGE STATE—MORE THAN FIVE TIMES AS BIG AS NEW YORK STATE!

So, U.S. troops in Texas had to **enforce** the order of the Emancipation Proclamation. Some people didn't follow the order because they didn't want to free Black Americans. So they continued to enslave them.

Even after Juneteenth, some white people in Houston, Texas, stopped Black Americans in the street and asked who "owned" them. They were sometimes put to work for the city.

There were about 250,000 enslaved people in Texas in 1865. Many were forced to work on large farms, like this one, which is now a museum about the history of slavery.

FUN FACT: 7

AS WORD OF GRANGER'S ORDER SPREAD, MANY BLACK AMERICANS CELEBRATED WITH SINGING, DANCING, AND PRAYING.

Celebrations were spontaneous, or unplanned. One formerly enslaved person, Felix Haywood, said, "Everybody went wild. We all felt like heroes ... just like that, we were free."

WHAT'S IN A NAME?

FUN FACT: 8

THE NAME "JUNETEENTH" IS A COMBINATION OF WORDS.

"June" and "Nineteenth" are combined to make "Juneteenth." The addition of "-teenth" also makes it sound like a **vague** date. This may be to show how slowly the news of freedom spread.

In modern times, people may celebrate Juneteenth by participating in rallies, or gatherings for a purpose, with the aim of preventing continued **racism**.

This statue, found at the Booker T. Washington National Monument, is called *Day of Jubilee*. The day a formerly enslaved person learned of their freedom was sometimes called their "day of jubilee."

FUN FACT: 9

THE HOLIDAY CELEBRATED ON JUNE 19 HAS HAD MANY NAMES OVER THE YEARS.

"Juneteenth" has been called Emancipation Day, Freedom Day, Black Independence Day, **Liberation** Day, and Jubilee Day. A jubilee is a yearly celebration of a special time.

MARKING THE DAY

FUN FACT: 10

FORMERLY ENSLAVED PEOPLE BUILT WHAT WERE CALLED "FREEDMAN'S TOWNS" IN TEXAS CITIES.

They built freedman's towns in Houston, Dallas, Austin, and San Antonio. The first official Juneteenth celebrations, in 1866, took place in these Texas cities. They included singing and food.

Freedman's towns included areas in Houston's Fourth Ward, shown here.

Enslavers often used clothing as a means of control. It meant a lot to get rid of it. This photo from Juneteenth 1900 shows people posing for a photo in their best clothing.

FUN FACT: 11

EARLY JUNETEENTH CELEBRATIONS SOMETIMES MEANT NEW CLOTHES.

New clothing **symbolized** freedom. In the earliest celebrations in Texas, some people threw the clothing they wore when they were enslaved into the river. They began a **tradition** of wearing new clothes.

PUBLIC SPACES

FUN FACT: 12

MANY GOVERNMENTS TRIED TO KEEP BLACK AMERICANS FROM GATHERING IN PUBLIC. BUT PEOPLE FOUND WAYS TO KEEP CELEBRATING!

The celebration of Juneteenth soon spread throughout the southern United States. However, some governments used so-called Black codes to limit Black people's freedoms. This included gatherings and the right to vote.

In response to Black codes, Juneteenth celebrations began to include efforts to empower Black people. Even today, many celebrations include voter **registration** drives.

This photo shows a Juneteenth celebration in 1880 in Emancipation Park.

FUN FACT: 13

MANY BLACK PEOPLE SAVED FOR AND BOUGHT LAND ON WHICH TO HOLD JUNETEENTH CELEBRATIONS.

Having land for gathering was important for Juneteenth. Sometimes the use of public spaces wasn't allowed. Black leaders in Houston, Texas, purchased Emancipation Park in 1872 for Juneteenth celebrations. These continue today!

TASTY TRADITIONS

FUN FACT: 14

MANY JUNETEENTH TRADITIONS INCLUDE FOOD, SUCH AS BARBECUE, BLACK-EYED PEAS, LEAFY GREENS, AND CORN.

Some of these foods are said to bring good luck or even wealth to those who eat them. Black-eyed peas, native to Africa, look a bit like eyes. They were thought to keep away evil spirits.

Some people think eating black-eyed peas brings good fortune, or luck. They eat them for New Year's celebrations too.

Hibiscus hot tea or iced tea is a traditional Juneteenth drink. Hibiscus is a plant that grows in West Africa.

FUN FACT: 15

RED FOODS ARE A JUNETEENTH TRADITION.

These may include strawberry soda, red velvet cake, and fruits such as strawberries and watermelon. The color red meant different things to different African peoples. For example, to the Yworuba and Kongo peoples, red meant power and change.

THE CELEBRATIONS SPREAD

FUN FACT: 16

TEXAS WAS THE FIRST STATE TO MAKE JUNETEENTH AN OFFICIAL STATE HOLIDAY IN 1980.

This was 115 years after U.S. soldiers first arrived in Galveston. Other states followed Texas. More U.S. cities hosted large celebrations. Countries including France and Ghana have also marked Juneteenth.

People take part in a Juneteenth parade in Philadelphia, Pennsylvania.

A MODERN JUNETEENTH TIMELINE

1960s:

Interest in Juneteenth celebrations grows during the **Civil Rights Movement.**

JUNE 19, 1968:

The Poor People's March, which had been planned by Dr. Martin Luther King Jr., takes place on Juneteenth in Washington, DC.

JANUARY 1, 1980:

Juneteenth becomes an official state holiday in Texas.

1994:

The movement to make Juneteenth a federal holiday begins.

2020:

The Black Lives Matter movement brings new attention to the push to make Juneteenth a federal holiday. The bill doesn't make it through the U.S. Congress.

JUNE 2021:

A new Juneteenth bill makes it through the Congress. President Joe Biden signs it into law on June 17.

JUNETEENTH HEROES

FUN FACT: 17

Edwards (1937–2020) was a freshman, or new, state **representative** in Texas when he put forth the bill to make Juneteenth a state holiday. After that, he worked to make it a national holiday for years.

Al Edwards was born in Houston, Texas. He was also involved in the Civil Rights Movement.

Vice President Kamala Harris stands to the left as Opal Lee speaks during a Juneteenth celebration in 2023 at the White House.

FUN FACT: 18

"GRANDMOTHER OF JUNETEENTH" OPAL LEE LED A WALK FROM TEXAS TO WASHINGTON, DC, TO GATHER SUPPORT FOR MAKING JUNETEENTH A NATIONAL HOLIDAY.

Lee was 89 years old in 2016 when she started her walk. "Surely somebody," she said, "would notice a little old lady in tennis shoes."

A FEDERAL HOLIDAY

FUN FACT: 19

The last new federal holiday was Martin Luther King Jr. Day in 1983. The Juneteenth bill passed the Senate with no "no" votes. It passed 415 to 14 in the House of Representatives.

Juneteenth became one of 12 federal holidays, which also include Memorial Day and Independence Day.

People watch as Biden signs the Juneteenth law.

FUN FACT: 20

WHEN JUNETEENTH BECAME A NEW FEDERAL HOLIDAY, THE UNITED STATES GAINED A SECOND INDEPENDENCE DAY!

The Juneteenth bill was signed into law June 17, 2021. It officially named the new holiday "Juneteenth National Independence Day." As President Joe Biden signed the bill, supporters including Opal Lee celebrated.

A BEGINNING

The push to make Juneteenth a federal holiday came to an end in 2021. In May 2021, a **poll** by the Gallup company showed that only 37 percent of Americans knew "a lot" or "some" about the holiday. By June 2022, about 59 percent knew about it. That number will likely grow.

Many hope that learning about Juneteenth will help others understand U.S. history better. "We don't want people to think that Juneteenth is a stopping point, because it isn't," Opal Lee said in October 2021. She called it a "beginning."

You might see the Juneteenth flag flying on this federal holiday. The star symbolizes Texas and Black Americans' freedom in all 50 states. The starburst lines around it symbolize "new beginnings."

GLOSSARY

celebration: A show of happiness for an event with special activities.

Civil Rights Movement: A time period in U.S. history starting in the 1950s in which African Americans fought for equal civil rights, or the freedoms granted to us by law.

culture: The beliefs and ways of life of a group of people.

enforce: To make a rule or law effective or active.

inform: To give facts and ideas. Information is facts and ideas.

liberation: The act of setting free.

poll: A questioning of people to get information. Also, a record of that information.

racism: The belief that people of different races have different qualities and abilities and that some are superior or inferior.

registration: The act of registering, or signing up, as a voter.

representative: A member of a lawmaking body who acts for voters.

symbolize: To serve as a symbol of, or to stand for something else.

tradition: A way of life or an action that a group of people has practiced for a long time.

vague: Not clearly stated.

BOOKS

Agostini, Alliah L. *The Juneteenth Story: Celebrating the End of Slavery in the United States.* Bellevue, WA: Becker and Mayer! Kids, 2022.

Garrett, Van G. *Juneteenth: A Picture Book for Kids Celebrating Black Joy.* New York, NY: Versify, 2023.

Jewel, Kirsti. *What Is Juneteenth?* New York, NY: Penguin Workshop, 2022.

WEBSITES

A Juneteenth Celebration
www.timeforkids.com/g56/a-juneteenth-celebration/
Learn more about how Juneteenth became a holiday at *Time for Kids.*

Celebrating Juneteenth
kids.nationalgeographic.com/history/article/celebrating-juneteenth
National Geographic Kids shares more about Juneteenth celebrations.

What Does Juneteenth Celebrate?
wonderopolis.org/wonder/What-Does-Juneteenth-Celebrate
Wonderopolis provides some Juneteenth information and activities.

INDEX